MY BROTHER MY SISTER

by Sue Mosteller

photographs by
Donna Moyseuik

GRIFFIN HOUSE
TORONTO 1974

©Sisters of St. Joseph, Toronto, 1972, 1974
©Donna Moyseuik, 1972, 1974

ISBN 0 88760 071 9
First published 1972
Second edition 1974

Published by Griffin Press Limited
461 King Street West, Toronto M5V 1K7, Canada

Text on page 88 is from *Something Beautiful for God*,
Malcolm Muggeridge, published in Canada by William Col-
lins Sons & Co. Cda., Ltd. and in the United States by
Harper & Row Publishers Inc.

Printed and bound in Canada by
The Alger Press Limited

Preface to the Second Edition

It is good to have this opportunity to express both my
surprise and my gratitude at the response to the first edition
of this book. My desire to share what was influencing me,
proved truly, to be an inspiration of the Spirit, for so many
wrote or told me that these simple lines had touched them.

Meanwhile I have been living as an assistant at Daybreak,
one of the L'Arche homes in Canada and today MY
BROTHER MY SISTER means more to me than when I
wrote it. Somehow there has been a transition from looking,
to living and growing into the reality expressed in these pages.

Sharing my life, these past two years, under the same roof
and at the same table, in work and in leisure with the
mentally and socially handicapped, my brothers and sisters,
has had its progressive stages. The honeymoon stage was
wonderful. Then the gradual discovery of the day to day
difficulties and the weaknesses in the system and in the
people. Next the questions; "What am I doing here?", "Is
my struggle worthwhile?", and "Is this really where I ought
to be?" Finally, in learning acceptance, a deepening of the
conviction that it is important for each of us to be here, doing
our share to make this community work. The experiences
of my own weakness, in trying to make it happen, in trying
to love, have brought some discouraging moments, but there
is most certainly a deepening in trust and hope.

And there is reason to hope. For throughout the world,
homes are springing up, where one finds brothers and
sisters trying to live together and trying to love one another.
In Canada nine homes have begun in the last two years,
while others have started in Scotland, England, India,
Belgium, Denmark and Africa.

There is much yet to be done. But our family is growing —
brothers and sisters of the same Father.

"Therefore I will proclaim You O Lord among the nations,
and I will sing praise to Your Name." Psalm 17; 50
S.M.   July, 1974

Preface to the First Edition

This book I desire to share with you,

    my brother, my sister.

Initially it was to introduce you more deeply to
    Jean Vanier, Mother Teresa.

    my brother, my sister.

Gradually, however,
they shared their friends with me.
    the assistants at L'Arche
    the Missionaries of Charity.

    brothers, sisters.

These, in their turn
introduced me in a new way to friends,
    the retarded, the dying in India,
    prisoners, the hungry,
    lepers, the destitute,

    brothers, sisters.

and,
linked mysteriously to all of the above
is another,
    Jesus,

    my brother.

S.M.   July, 1972

'Blessed are the poor,' He says.

'I was a stranger and you took me in.'

'Love your enemies.'

Humanly speaking this is not possible.
        The poor are not blessed.
        The stranger I do not welcome.
        The enemy is precisely the one
        I do not love.

This message is not meant to be a
        human possibility,
because He gives us His Spirit,
the Master of the impossible.

The Spirit leaves us no loopholes
if we desire to answer the call to
        universal brotherhood.

'God chose what is foolish in the world
        to shame the wise.
God chose what is weak in the world
        to confound the strong.'
                (I Corinthians, 1:27)

Mother Teresa Boyaxhiu is an Albanian nun living in India, and foundress of the Community of the Missionaries of Charity, whose work it is to serve the poorest of the poor in the world.

"Faith is a gift of God. Without it there would be no life. And our work, to be fruitful and to be all for God, and beautiful, has to be built on faith. Faith in Christ who said, 'I was hungry, I was naked, I was sick, and I was homeless and you did that to me.' On these words of his, all our work is based."
(Mother Teresa, Something Beautiful For God
by Malcolm Muggeridge)

Mother Teresa is foolish
    is weak,

      to think that she, a foreigner, and alone
      could alleviate, to any extent,
      the vast sufferings in Calcutta,

and

      to have to depend upon the poor
      to accept her,
      then, once accepted,
      to have to depend upon the rich
      to support her.

Mother Teresa, founder of
the Missionaries of Charity

My initial contact with Mother Teresa
     spelled joy.
She said so little.

It was a long distance call
     Toronto to Rome.
I said, 'We want you to come to Toronto
with Jean Vanier when you are in Washington
next week. It's about three hours by plane.
We've rented a hall and we want you to meet
our young people. We'll look after all the
practical details of your coming.
Will you come?'

She answered, 'Yes.
I'm bringing five Sisters from India that day
to open a house in Harlem, but I think I could
be finished in the early afternoon. Could you
call Miss Egan in New York and check details
with her? I'll speak with you more when we meet.'

We thanked each other and hung up.

Our young people said her visit was
     joy and hope and challenge.
For me, it was a calling forth to
     share the inspiration.

When this book became a reality, I travelled to
India to meet with her. By her welcome I knew
that she was prepared to help as much as
possible.

I wanted to capture every word. I had my pad
and pencil ready; hopeful, poised.
I asked, 'If you are not paid for your work,
how do the Sisters live?'

She answered, 'The Lord looks after us.'

It wasn't hard to get every word!

One of the Sisters,
Calcutta, India

Words were not to be the only source
of our communication.
Answers to my questions came
through the eyes, the attitude,
the whole quality of the presence,
by the witness of the lives
of those seven hundred Sisters.

But something else.
The questions themselves
seemed to disintegrate
before an eruption of
deeper, more profound questionings
about the nature of an old, old concept,
MERCY.

That word, that attitude
has been clothed with flesh
and is alive,
and beautiful,
and possible.

Jean Vanier is a Canadian layman, living in France and founder of L'Arche, an international community to create homes with mentally retarded adults.

"At L'Arche we are trying to establish small homes of eight handicapped men or boys and one or two assistants. It is a question of creating an atmosphere where mentally handicapped men and women can live their lives as happily as possible; working, making the most of their time of leisure, developing according to the deepest aspirations of their being. It is a question of creating a truly human community where they can find the necessary security in order to progress in every human and spiritual domain; particularly where their hearts can be allowed freely to develop in love for their brothers and for God; a place where they can taste the eternal joys, often silent and peaceful, of a fraternal life in the presence of Jesus."

(Jean Vanier, Eruption to Hope)

Jean Vanier is foolish, too
    is weak,

to spend years, studying Philosophy and
    Theology only to go and live with
    retarded people, and

to have to depend upon the Spirit
    to send people to help,
    to bind the community in love.

    "Community can only be created
    and nurtured and strengthened
    by the deep, transforming power
    of the Holy Spirit.
    Humanly speaking,
    this is not possible."

(Jean Vanier)

Jean Vanier and
Raphael at L'Arche

My contact with Jean Vanier
        has been something else,
best explained in the words
        community and
        poverty.

Working with him on projects,
has meant sharing his resources,
namely,
        his friends.

Community implies openness and welcome,
        acceptance and creativity,
qualities I find not only in Jean,
        but in the many friends he shares with me.

With some, like Francoise, at L'Arche,
        I have no common language.
With others, like Willie May in the Hough Ghetto
        of Cleveland,
        I share only a small measure of understanding.
Those I've met with Jean in the penitentiaries,
        or in hospitals
        or in the ghettoes of Chicago, Washington,
        Cleveland and New York
are teaching me another set of values,
        difficult to confine in words.
It has to do with
        the poverty of all my riches.

The wounds are sometimes deep.
My fear is great.
Some of these brothers and sisters
        may become violent
or they may already have retreated
into another world,
        the world of fantasy
        of dream.
Thus, we cannot always relate
        to one another.

But this community of friends is,
by the discovery method,
        teaching me.
My discovery is disconcerting;
there is so much to learn.

I still say in principle,
'Blessed are the rich, the powerful.'
But they help me to discover the
'Blessedness of the poor.'

I identify with
'Love friends, be merry.'
While they remind me,
'Love your enemies, the unlovable ones.'

It doesn't make sense
nor is it possible.
Besides, it is absurd.

And yet I discover
        the Spirit.
The One, Who
makes the impossible
        possible,
and the absurd
        sensible.

"The beautiful thing about Jesus
is, that he never calls us alone.

When Jesus says, 'Come, come,'
to Philip and Andrew,
then Andrew goes to Peter and says,
'We have found the Messiah.'

Philip goes to Nathanial and says,
'We have found the peacemaker.'

So it is when He gives us his Spirit;
he very quickly creates a family.

He gives us brothers and sisters,
the spirit of brotherhood and love.
He creates in us a union
which means that
our hearts beat in unison,
motivated by the same yearnings,
the same hopes,
the same aspirations."

(Jean Vanier)

Dinner at the Hermitage
(a L'Arche home in France)

The Community of the Missionaries of Charity
and the communities of L'Arche
    share certain common characteristics,
    joy
    openness
    welcome
    love.
Basically, however the communities are not similar.

The Missionaries of Charity are a traditional, religious order of the Church. Young people come with a desire to consecrate their lives to Jesus in the distressing disguise of poverty. They undertake an intensive novitiate training in spiritual formation. Their life is structured in such a way that wherever they are sent, through obedience to work, their life-style remains unchanged. They are committed to rise early, pray together, read spiritual books, recreate together and live apart from those they serve. Each take the same vows, obedience, chastity, poverty and charity and each comes to serve for life. In extreme situations where there is danger and suffering, they endeavour to become present, and to remedy insofar as they are able, the sources of distress.

L'Arche is not a religious community of the Church. Assistants do not come for life. Basically, its work is not in the extreme situations, but in the gradual calling forth to life; like the blossoming of a flower.

"The communities of L'Arche are diverse, rather like the Church. Not one group of people all the same, not even one form or type of spirituality, but men and women from all horizons, the fervent and the non-fervent, the traditional and the avant-garde, each bearing in his being the marks of different forms of handicap. Some deep believers, others, groping in the dark. Some attracted for social reasons, some, just to pray, but all united in some immense growth, urging each other forward to greater love and attention. The Spirit guiding gently through tears and laughter, orienting these strange communities of disfigured people, believing in the Disfigured One."

(Jean Vanier)

'But Mother Teresa, you don't understand,'
    said the New York businessman.
'Do you realize what this means?
It may be all right in India,
    but Harlem is different!
You can't just bring Sisters in here
    when they have no income.
You can't expect that they will live
    and eat,
    and be able to do anything worthwhile
    if they do not accept a salary of some kind.
This is not possible.
What are you thinking of?'

And with her little smile,
'I'm only thinking that this is the pattern
    of our lives.
We take no money for our work.
When the Lord stops giving to us,
    we will stop giving to the poor.
Also, I'm thinking, that
    if Our Lord is to go bankrupt,
    He probably won't do it in New York City!'

One of the Sisters,
Calcutta home for abandoned children

Harlem is one of our open wounds;
        the culmination of decades of suffering,
        exploitation, indifference,
        smouldering hatred,
        flaring violence.

Most of us,
        the vast majority,
have never been present there.

The ancient ruins of the old world
        have been captured on our cameras.
But our feet have never walked, or stopped
        beside the broken and the wounded
        of our own cities.

Fear prevents us.

We have so much to lose.

'We choose to be poor,' Mother Teresa says.
'Jesus, being rich, became poor for the
love of us,
so as to be able to understand
        who the poor are,
        how the poor feel when they are poor,
        and how difficult it is for them to be poor.
We try to live their poverty or want. I do not
know how the work in Harlem will start or continue,
but I know that these five Sisters will try to give
love,
and nothing else.'

Sister Andrea visits families in Harlem.

The women speak with her about the
one parent family situations there, the
absentee landlords, the welfare, housing,
and health problems, learning disabilities
of their children, and discrimination.

She sees the impossibility of the total
situation; children being caught up into the
circle of hatred and despair, of ignorance
and poverty.

Sister wants to be there, even though she
can admit that her small efforts are quickly
swallowed in the vast arena of despair. She
has opted not to make loud protestations about
injustice. She is not so good at public
speaking. She does not carry banners in the
streets, knowing that this is sometimes an
excuse for not being present to the suffering.
She does not plan to go away and do research
on the problems of the ghetto. It is important
for her to be there, present to the poor,
but believing that these suffering brothers
and sisters are children of the same Father
and worthy of her life.

The district is known for its hostility.
Yet the Sisters walk the streets to visit
their people. Danger is everywhere, but
so is suffering. Somewhere, a mother
waits for her friend to come, a light in
that world of darkness and despair.

She will come.

In Trosly-Breuil, a tiny village north of Paris, Père Thomas was chaplain at Le Val Fleuri, a home for thirty retarded men. When he heard from Jean Vanier about his desire to begin a small community for retarded adults, he liked the idea and welcomed Jean to the village.

The Père is an enigma,
    an utter contradiction,
yet his influence in the unfolding
of L'Arche
has been deeply significant.

He is a man, called to contemplation,
    to silence, and poverty and union with God.
He is detached in many ways,
    independent of the others.

But he is not a retired hermit.

Rather, his presence,
    his gentleness,
    his love for the wounded ones
    and for the assistants,
    for Jean,
    and for the Lord Jesus,
    permeates L'Arche.

Philippe and Pere John,
L'Arche, Trosly Breuil, France

Jean began simply. He bought a house
and moved in with Louis, his friend from
Montreal, Raphael and Phillippe, two men
from the psychiatric hospital. Both of
the latter had lived many years in the
hospital without the hope of ever leaving.
The house was old and delapidated so together
they began to rebuild and redecorate it.
They called it L'Arche.

Jean tells that initially he was certain
he would never have more than four men, so
it would be possible to travel and do things
together as a group. This neat little plan
was fortunately doomed to a short life span.

Soon Henri arrived. Then Gerry and Anne-Marie
came to the workshop. Anne-Marie's sister,
Annie followed not long after. With all
this help, they were able to welcome Jacques
and Pierrot. Then Marie-Benoit came for the
kitchen, to nourish this newly born family.
Students knocked on the door, to look or to
work, hearing of L'Arche from Jean who
occasionally came to Canada to give talks.

Just down the road Le Val Fleuri, the large
home with many handicapped, was having
administrative difficulties. This home
was not Jean's idea of a L'Arche community,
but when he was invited to take it over,
he agreed because of the small village
surroundings, the growing numbers of assistants,
and the links of friendship growing between
the Père and the men of both communities.

Studying in Europe, Steve and Ann, Canadians, came to open a new foyer, Les Rameaux, in Trosly. Later they returned to Canada and with the help of friends began Daybreak House. With Fred, their son, and several assistants, they live with wounded men and women from the surrounding area.

Gradually, gradually people came and houses were opened and the wounded welcomed. Sometimes the assistants move on and out of contact. Some move on, maintaining the links of friendship. Others move on and make beginnings elsewhere, and still others, remain.

A school of special educators sent Agnes to work at the Val. While there she met Adrianno, from Portugal, who had been studying in Canada and had come to help for the summer. Later, they were married and now, with Emmanual, their small son, they direct the foyers and workshops at La Merci, a large farm in southwest France.

Geoffrey and Ann came to Canada from England to work with Steve and Ann. Now they are home, working with Therese on the L'Arche to be opened soon in England, near Canterbury.

Frank and Anne-Marie and their four children sold their house recently and have moved to a farm outside Montreal. They have visited a nearby institution and soon hope to welcome some of the handicapped adults from there to share their home. They have never been to L'Arche; proof that the Spirit is not confined to Trosly. L'Arche becomes possible anywhere, at any time, linked to Trosly or not, when men open their hearts and homes to their wounded brothers and sisters.

And all the while, as L'Arche grows,
    Père Thomas is quietly there.
Maybe you won't notice him
    if you don't come to Mass,
Or maybe you'll see him
    bicycling down a street in Trosly,
    his Dominican robes flowing in the wind,
    his beret almost inside out,
    He may even be unshaven.

He speaks quietly.
Some find his sermons long,
    but all listen to the music of his word,
    calling,
    calling forth to silence and prayer.

    ''A strong heart
    throbbing
    at the heart of
    the community.''
                   (Jean Vanier)

Pere Don and Pere Thomas —
the chapel at L'Arche

"After working twenty years
    among the dying, the sick, the crippled,
    the handicapped, and mentally deficient
    men, women, and children,
I have come to one conclusion only,
as I have tried to feel with the people
    their suffering,
I have come to the understanding
    of what Jesus felt
    when he came amongst his own
    and they didn't want him."
                    (Mother Teresa)

With the lepers
in Bangalore, India

Children,
there are so many children in need.

    Some are abandoned on the doorstep,
    Others, found in the streets.

Infants, with tiny heads
        and old, old faces,
        and eyes that speak,
        sadness.

Some are premature and will die.

But they will not leave this world,
        unloved.
Others, who should be dead,
    have survived.

The children's home, –
Madras, India

The Missionary Brothers have a house
        for homeless boys,
some of whom are found in the streets,
        orphaned,
or others who have lived and slept
        and stolen food
on the railway platform of Calcutta.

The Brothers simply try to provide
        for their immediate needs,
sharing their meagre resources
        with the children.

Their friend, the psychiatrist
        is a support and a strength
for they are inexperienced,
        especially with the retarded
        or emotionally disturbed.

A Missionary Brother
with homeless boys – Calcutta

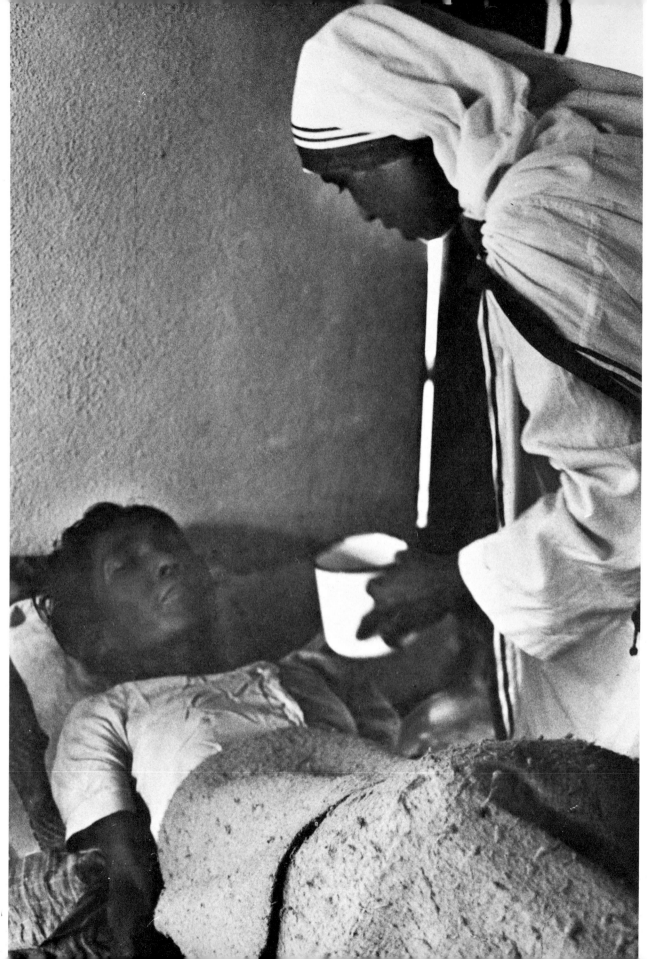

'I cannot speak of myself,' Mother Teresa told me,
    'for the situation is all one.
Without the poor and their acceptance
    I would not be here.
Without the Sisters, the Co-workers, and the Friends,
    I would not be here.

To be here, is to need.
    I need the Sisters.
    They need me.
    The poor need us.
    We need them.
You see, it is all together.'

I had said to her,

'Your work must be very attractive.
You have seven hundred sisters
    in twenty years;
also, one hundred brothers!
And in this difficult time
    you have two hundred novices!'

She quickly corrected me.

'No! The work is not attractive,
but many young people today are
beginning to see how beautiful the
    poor are.'

The House of the Dying —
Calcutta

If there are questions for Mother Teresa
about bringing Sisters to Harlem,
there are likewise questions for Jean Vanier
starting a community for the handicapped
in India.

'In many ways,'
he wrote in the Letters of L'Arche,
'this new foundation in India can appear
     ridiculous . . .
to go all the way to Asia to begin a home
when there is such need here in France and in Canada.
What sense can there be
     in such a foundation,
in a country so far away,
     where we do not even know the language
     and where we are in many ways
     so unarmed for the work?
If I let myself be taken in by human prudence,
the new foundation seems non-sensical.
However, with great rapidity,
     Gabrielle, Mira and myself
were able to establish deep friendships
     with many important and responsible people
and with them, we opened our first 'Asha Niketan.'

It is the rapidity with which all this
     was done
that made me understand
     the folly of human prudence
     which is frequently temerity,
and to see the wisdom of audacity
     in the light of the Spirit
which seeks to cross frontiers
     in order to attain those who are suffering
     the world over.'

Zizi, Daisy, George and Lennie –
a L'Arche home in Kotigiri, India

Yoga at Asha Niketan,
a L'Arche home in Bangalore

Gabrielle, from Germany, is responsible for
the first home of hope, Asha Niketan, established
in India in 1970. She left L'Arche to take over
the house that disciples of Gandhi had put at the
community's disposal, near Bangalore.

Guru smiles. He has a few English words,
but mostly he speaks Kannada. Guru was
one of the first men to join Gabrielle, so
he is a little like the ancient of the community,
welcoming newcomers and friends.

Shrinivasan radiates joy. He, too, loves
to welcome people, clasp their hand and
show them about the house. Not so a year
ago when he first came to join the community
from the mental hospital. His early days
were marred by fits and tantrums,
by biting and scratching. Gradually he has
met friends and his outbursts are becoming
fewer and fewer. He seems to be finding a
home and much to rejoice about.

John too, bears wounds in his mind and
in his heart. His gift to the world is
a smile and a manner that radiates peace.
Returning to Asha Niketan after a weekend
with his mother, he accidentally boarded the
wrong bus and disappeared. His friends
were aware that there was very little chance
of ever finding him. Nevertheless, they
published his picture in the local newspapers,
made innumerable inquiries and prayed.

One evening, a month later, a stranger
called and gave a vague location, about
thirty miles away, where he thought he
had recognized the man from the newspaper.

Ron and Judy arrived in the general vicinity
about midnight. The darkness, their own
unfamiliarity with the region, and the vision
of many hundreds of poor people, sleeping
by the roadside, did nothing to boost their
hopes of finding John. But at a given moment
Judy suggested they simply stop and inquire.
When Ron got out and walked a few paces,
he found himself looking into the large blue
eyes of none other than John, thirty pounds
lighter, pale and weak.

John smiled and said, 'Yes, home,' to Ron's
question, 'would you like to stay here or come
home with us?'

Apparently his homeless brothers had given
him food and kept him alive.

Genuine concern for his recovery followed
the rejoicing of his homecoming.

Judy worked for a year at L'Arche,
then returned to Canada to get her Reg.N.
Last year she joined Gabrielle, Ron,
Saroja and the boys at Asha Niketan in India.

The simplicity of life, the language
difficulties, the change of diet and the
work have been new to her. She has
adapted sufficiently to cope with the
mosquitoes and to do without fans in
the intense heat. Besides this, the
limitations of her budget have opened
her to the experiences of shopping
for bargains in the market and
travelling third class on the Indian trains!
Indescribable!

She spoke of her life at Asha Niketan.

'I really miss the family, I guess because
I'm so far from them. But I just know that
for the present, this is where I must be.
The work itself is quite boring, but the
boys are wonderful and I experience a lot of
peace just being with them. I struggle
along with my own difficulties, trying to
follow Jesus and be where I must be.
For the most part, I am peaceful.'

Shrivas, Guru and Judy
water the trees – Bangalore

Zizi

When we arrived at Stonehouse, in the Blue Mountains,
Zizi, a young Canadian assistant, dropped the
trousers she was mending for Lennie, and ran to
embrace us. Then Mira and Tom, the responsibles,
welcomed us and introduced us to Lennie, George
and Daisy.

Mira, who worked in Trosly for six years or more,
married Tom last year and together they have
started the second home of hope, Asha Niketan,
Stonehouse, in southern India.

Lennie and George were sent to them by Mother
Teresa in Calcutta, because their mother, 75,
had been admitted to the house of the dying.
These men are twins, thirty seven years of age
and both mentally retarded.

We went with them for tea to a convent of Irish nuns
who welcomed us heartily, but really only had eyes for
Lennie and George. The way they served them, with
such delicacy and respect, was beautiful.

Lennie told them about their friend from Calcutta.

>   'Mother Teresa is really kind.
>   She always stopped to talk
>   to us. She goes into the streets
>   you know, to pick up old and lonely
>   people.
>   She's fond of my brother George and I.'

Daisy and I stopped to buy eggs on our way home. The
proprietor used a small paper bag, made from cut and
glued newspaper. Tom, and the men had made the bags
at Asha Niketan, Stonehouse.

Creating a new community cannot be accomplished
without difficulties and sufferings. Since we were there,
Mira has taken ill and Asha Niketan, Stonehouse, for
the present, has had to be closed. Lennie and George
have moved to Asha Niketan in Bangalore.

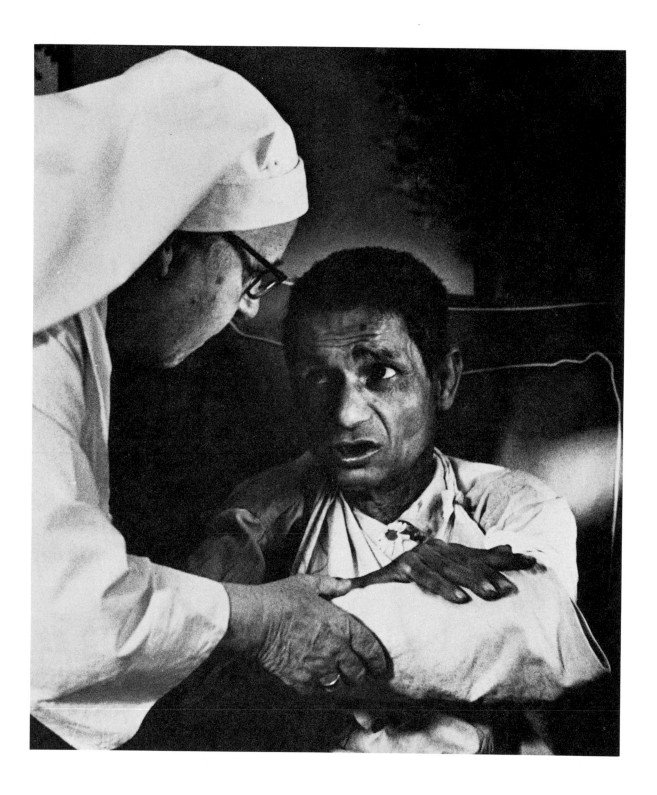

"God, save us at every step
　　from being too well established,
　　from closing our hearts,
　　from defending our position . . .
Save us from neat little projects
　　meant to save a certain number of cases
　　that 'we' have chosen to handle,
if they immunize us against any other brother
　　whose unexpected call for food,
　　for recognition, for justice,
　　for friendship, for love,
be he rich or poor,
　　upsets our little peace."

(Gabrielle: Letters of L'Arche 1971)

*One of the Sisters
with Lennie – Kotigiri*

*In the streets
of Calcutta*

"Once you know Calcutta
        you can never leave it for good.
There is that strange attraction,
        that immense crowd of paupers,
        a city of death and of life.
It is a triumph of life over death,
        masses of derelicts,
        alive and smiling,
        sleeping, lamenting.
A city where great love exists between
        people.
        The poor are good to the poor,
        so many acts of charity,
        of mutual help, of kindness;
so many who are in a state of misery,
        but who forget their misery to
        help one who is more miserable yet."
                                    (Brother Andre)

Dashing down the crowded sidewalk, a
twelve year old boy collided with one of the
Missionaries, who held him with her eyes
momentarily, realizing that he had stolen
something. He was frightened, but when
she did not condemn him, he was able
to speak about himself.

He had never been to school. A man in the
park had taught him to steal. Each afternoon
he and others like himself met the man
and were directed where to go and what to
take. Failure to return with the goods meant
no money and often a beating.

Sister met him again. Again they spoke of
his life and livelihood. Would he like to
go to school? Would his companions come?
Where did he sleep? Could she visit his mother?

Gradually, out of this incident, the slum
school began. One of the parish schools
gave over their facilities after hours.
The children began to upgrade themselves,
with the help of the teachers and the sisters.

As they progressed the Sisters planned for
their future, so that now, once upgraded,
the children enter regular private schools,
sponsored by a co-worker in another land or
by a friend of the Missionaries. Thus, they
may complete their education, mingling with
children from richer backgrounds and competing
on a somewhat equal footing.

Two thousand children have been or are
presently being sponsored in this way.

Waiting
for medications
at the dispensary

At DumDum, a complex on the outskirts of Calcutta,
we met the Australian nurse, a co-worker, in the
house of the Dying. She was dressing the ulcerous
sores for one of the women and she paused to speak
with us. The sick woman too, greeted us with,
    'Namaste.'
Two Missionary Brothers were lifting a sick man
into a wheelchair, to take him for some sun.
He was very ill, but he welcomed us.

Some children, playing about followed us inside
to meet the sick ones in their cribs. They have all
been sick, close to death, from hunger and disease.
Many were crippled and some retarded, but the ones
who followed us and held our hands were living
signs of hope for all the others.

This, the Kennedy Centre, came to be, because
Mother Teresa was awarded a grant by the Joseph
P. Kennedy Jr. Foundation for outstanding service
to her fellow man.

Mother Teresa walks over the site with the
city planner from Calcutta.
The home for retarded children is almost finished.
The Home for sick and abandoned babies is operative.
The House of the Dying is well-occupied and the
dispensary, busy.

Seeing the many people lining up for medicines
    in the hot sun,
these two speak of changes;
put a roof here, move the line-up over there,
put a walkway here and so on.
Then spotting a tiny garden, Mother Teresa says,
'But don't do anything till we harvest the onions!'

Mother Teresa speaks with
the school children – Dum Dum

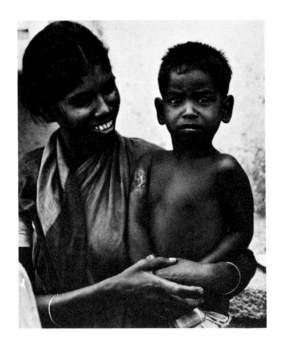

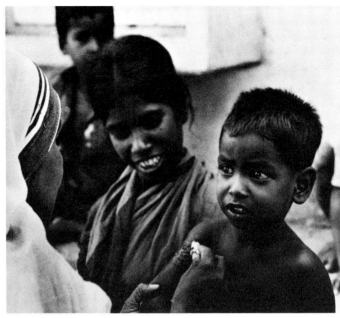

*The mobile dispensary
of the Missionary Sisters*

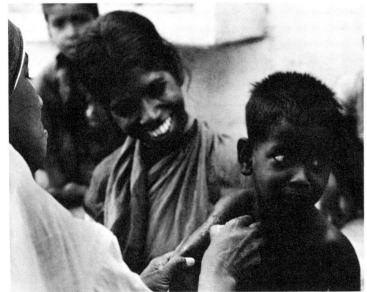

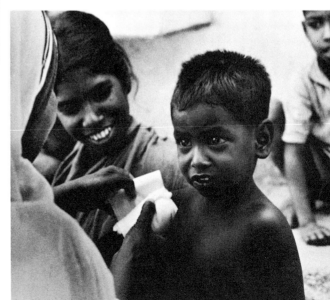

In order to be one with their suffering
brothers and sisters in India, some
families in England do without one meal
a week. With the money collected they have
purchased six vans for the Missionaries.

These mobile dispensaries go to a different
station each day, parking in a spot that
will insure some shade for those lining up
to receive medicines.

One sister in the front passenger seat
renews prescriptions or changes them.
Two others dispense the medications from
the back doors of the van. Pills are dispensed
in small envelopes, made from old newspapers,
folded into a sack. Pills for stomach disorders
are scarce. Vitamins and pain killers are
constants. Cough syrup is poured into the
empty, clean bottle that the poor person
has brought with him.

The poor are fearful, but patient, understanding
so little about medicine. The Sisters' patience
is even more, day after day, explaining,
comforting, listening, encouraging, dispensing,
especially peace and love.

In the realms of mercy,
    the healing is very deep.

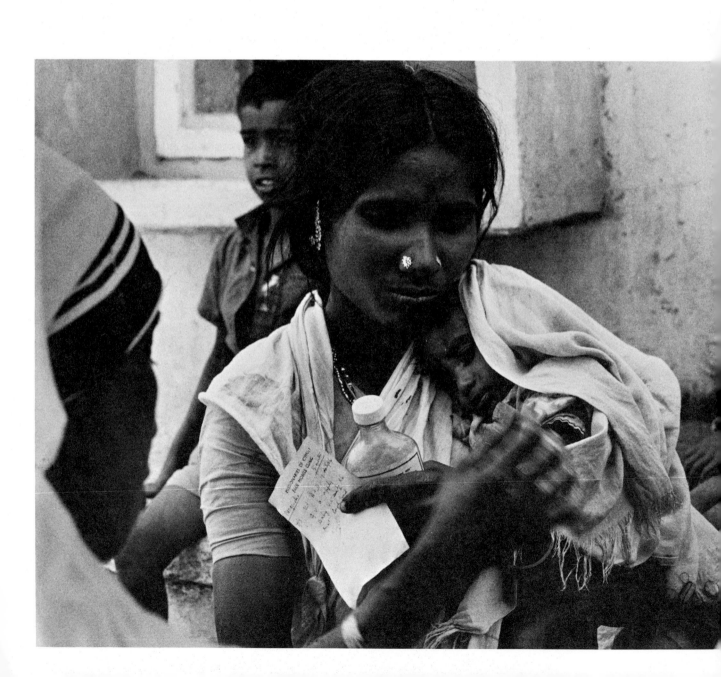

"In Calcutta and in many other places
    we see so much suffering,
    living suffering
    suffering that cannot be relieved just
    with a plate of rice,
    or a loaf of bread,
a suffering much deeper.

I think of Christ,
    coming amongst His own
and His own,
    didn't want Him."

(Mother Teresa)

The mobile dispensary

*Fred – the garden
at L'Arche in France*

One day at the supper table at L'Arche the
conversation turned to the question of salary:

'It's never enough,' one man said,
and
'I could use more,' said another.

Père Clarke listened for a time, then
began to question some of the more vocal
dissenters:
'Do you like your work?' he asked.

'Certainly,' was the reply.

'Are you happy when you're working?' he repeated.

'Of course, I love it. Sometimes I feel I
could work all day and all night,' another
answered.

'Then you should think about that,'
said the Père. 'It isn't the money after
all. You should be glad to be working where
you are busy and happy. You see the money
isn't important. It's the work. That's
the important thing.'

Pierrot had been listening — quietly.
Now he interrupts, leans over and advises:

'Ah non, mon père, the thing that is most
important after all is,
the rose.'

Jeanne Francois, Claude, Isabelle, Jean Pierre, Maurice at work
La Promesse, Pierrefonds, France

Michel at the mosaic workshop – Trosly, France

The gardens of La Merci – Cognac, France

Pierrot had said something quite profound,
for the rose and all it signifies is
related to the question of work at L'Arche.

Jean Vanier often speaks of the 'double' wound
suffered by the retarded man.
There is the organic wound from a given combination
of genes or from an accident at birth.
But the second wound is much greater —
rejection.

One form of rejection is the handicapped man's
inability to find work.

As opposed to the dreadful idleness suffered
by so many of the handicapped, sitting
alone or rocking on the floor,
the men and women at L'Arche work for
a small salary. Building, decorating,
ironworks, ceramics, book binding,
sub-contracting, factory work, kitchen and
house cleaning jobs are available.

Initially, one of the greatest obstacles
is the handicapped person's lack of self-
confidence and confidence in others.
It rises from having been told repeatedly
in so many subtle ways:
'You are deficient.' 'You can't do it.'

Gradually though, through the work and through
the belief of the assistants in the handicapped
man's potential, the épanouissement — the
blossoming — the rose comes into being.

Unlike the Missionaries of Charity who
take no money for their works, L'Arche
utilizes government funds wherever they
are available to found homes and workshops and to partially staff them with
paid professionals. But permanent pro-
fessional and non-professional voluntary
help is also welcomed and encouraged
among those who express that desire.

JoJo – La Merci

"I believe that everyone has a personal charisma,
        even the very, very handicapped.
You will find that those who are handicapped
        can do fantastic things.
When we are in front of the handicapped
our whole role is to show them
        the fantastic things they can do.

Jean Claude is beautiful. He is not going
to do any work, or very little, because he is
thirty now, but he has a great role in leisure.
He'll be the fellow, who will get up and give
speeches at table and make everyone laugh.

It's important that we help him recognise his
value, so he becomes conscious of his mission
in that community.

'So we don't say to him,'
'You're doing a great job of work,'
if he isn't doing a good job.
Instead we might say,
'You're a really good person. You know
we need you in this community. You make everyone
laugh and you have such good spirits. When you
are sad, everyone else is sad.'

Gradually he becomes conscious of his personal
        charisma.
He begins to realize that he is really needed.
He has a place to bring people hope and joy.

But this we can't always see straight away.
With some of the fellows it takes two or three
years before we begin to see what his particular
charisma is, within this specific community."
                              (Jean Vanier)

Bernard and Simone in the workshop in Trosly

The day Norbert, at La Petite Source,
'revolted' was the day the assistants who live
with him rejoiced.

Norbert is extra shy. Retarded at birth,
he was always treated by his parents as
a tiny baby who could do nothing. His entry
into L'Arche as an adult was painful.
He sat in the corner, his face to the wall,
or rode his bike into the forest to be alone.
At the foyer, each man is responsible for
some of the work. Norbert was trained to set
the table and with a little help in the
area of counting plates and forks, he
faithfully did his job for three years.
He was almost too good, never complaining, never
an extrovert.

Then one day at meal time, he didn't come.
They waited, but finally Elizabeth went
to his room.

Norbert was ready. 'No,' he affirmed.
'Why always me?'

Elizabeth explained once more how each
man has his responsibilities. If he didn't
like to set the table, he should talk to Sue,
the 'résponsable', about getting a change.

The next day he did just that, and now he
happily rinses the dishes each night.

The assistants rejoiced because Norbert, for
the first time in his life, asserted himself.
This is a landmark.

The kitchen at La Merci, Cognac

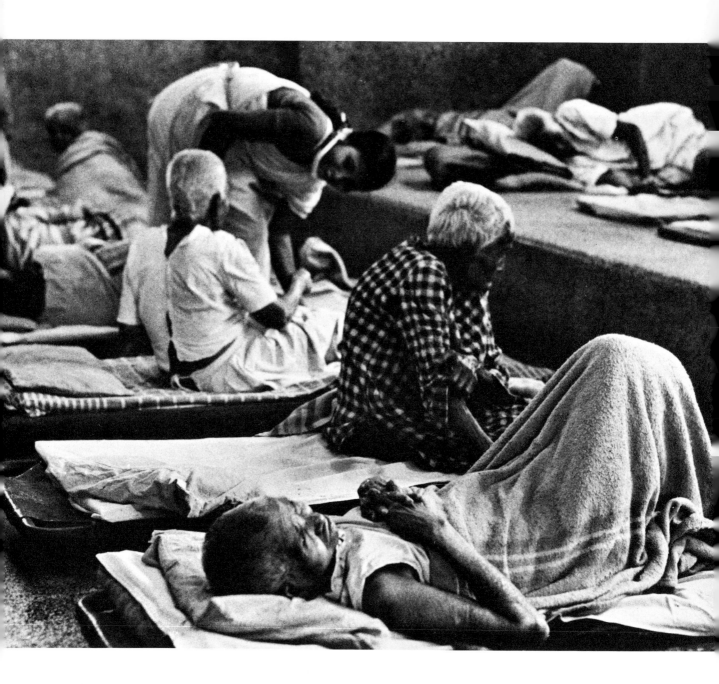

The Sisters so beautifully live their fourth vow;
   to give wholehearted,
   free service
   to the poorest of the poor,
in the House of the Dying,
where mercy and misery embrace.

To be admitted, one must be poor and ill and rejected.
The facilities are primitive indeed, two large rooms
with mats very close together for about 150
   ill and dying.

The atmosphere, for the most part, is peaceful
amid all this suffering and pain. Contrary to
the efficiency of a North American hospital, the
Sisters do not work with haste and precision;
rather with a look of compassion and an attitude
which says:
   'What is your suffering?'

The poor, many lying on mats in a lamentable state,
portray a remarkable acceptance of their sufferings,
realizing that they have been spared the terrors
of death alone, in misery, perhaps to be eaten by
the rats or the dogs. Here they may die in a place
of peace, surrounded with love and care,
a presence, radiating,
   'I believe in you and want to hear who you are.'

The Sisters go empty handed to the miserable ones,
believing in the immense possibility of the human
person, who by a hand, a smile, eyes,
   can give life.

In the women's section
The House of the Dying, Calcutta

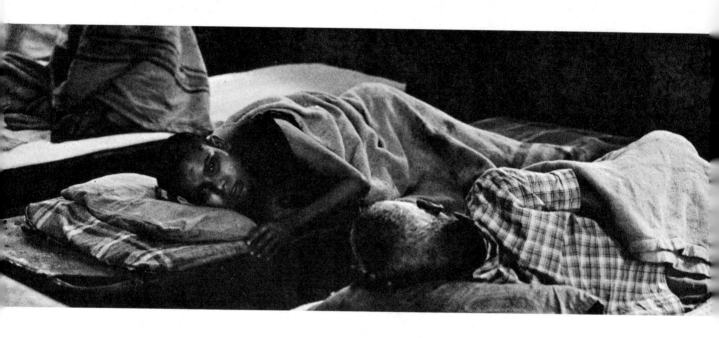

In the house of the dying
there is so much suffering of the heart.
There is no one,
no one to love them,
but the Sisters love them.
They smile and wash and clean them;
they are so good,
a presence of peace in the midst of
disease, cancer, V.D., T.B., and other things!

"One day a man was brought in
screaming and yelling.
He didn't want to die.
His backbone was broken in three places,
and he had many terrible ulcers.
His pain was intense.
He didn't want to see the Sisters.
He didn't want to die.

He was given morphine and love
in generous doses,
and he was told of the sufferings of One
who loved him very much.

Gradually he began to listen
and to accept love.
On his last day, he refused the morphine
because he wanted to be united to the One
who saved him."

(Mother Teresa)

During the afternoon rest period

Sister Agatha showed us the register of the house of the dying in Calcutta. Listed were the names of 26,055 patients.

'Over half of these people have died. Some who get better have no place to go, so they stay on to help. It takes a long time to get better, for our people have never had regular meals and care. In Calcutta, there is no place for them when they get better. They return to the streets, to beg.'

"For me each one is an individual.
I can give my whole heart to that person
        for that moment,
        in an exchange of love.

It is not social work.
We must love each other.
It involves emotional involvement
        making people feel they are wanted.

People today are in such a rush, in such
a big hurry,
but there are those,
        falling on both sides of the road
        because they cannot keep up.
        They are left alone.
These are the people to whom we must go,

One man was picked up and brought to the
        house of the dying.
He grasped the blankets and exclaimed
weakly:
        'Thank God, I can die like a human being.'

We cannot always save the life,
        but we can help them to die
        loved, cared for, wanted,
        like a human being."
                                    (Mother Teresa)

Assisting the dying

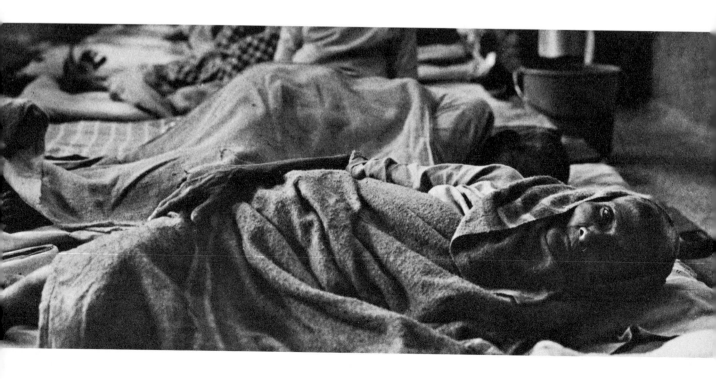

"Jesus, when he died said,
        'My God, my God, why have you forsaken me?'

Death is one of those fantastic passages where
        there is great agony.
The agony of death is an agony of separation.

One of the reasons why we reject others is
        that we do not want to assume the reality of death.
We are frightened of death,
        because death is that terrible thing
        which says to us:
        'What are you doing in front of this?
        all your possessions, all the money you have,
        all the cars you have, your egoism; this is nothing.
This is a bubble that one day will burst.'

So, death is one of those realities
        that pushes us back against the wall;
We are frightened of it.
That's why we don't want to look at our suffering
brothers
        who remind us of death."

(Jean Vanier)

In The House of the Dying

On Easter this year, some from L'Arche
pushed the 'community' bus to get it
started, then set out for a picnic. We
feasted, made speeches, sang and danced in
open air, then gathered for the celebration
of Mass.

At communion time, most of the 70 people
began to shuffle and arrange themselves in
a line before the altar.

Jean Michel waited for the group to settle
then called out for all to hear:

'Bon appétit pour le Bon Dieu!
Have a good appetite for the Lord!'

Almost home at 10:30 P.M., in the depth of
the Compeigne forest, the bus broke down.
It was a very black night in a very black
forest as we disembarked and began to
climb the hill out of range of the head-
lights. Then more fun began, as some
ran ahead to hide beside the road, then
jump out of the forest and scare us
half to death! Amid the screaming, we
heard the cry to come back and help push
the bus up the hill. In no time, we were
seated again, riding merrily home.

Easter Day Picnic, L'Arche

When Daybreak from Canada arrived in
Lourdes, France,
Peter observed carefully the surroundings
        and remarked,
'There sure are a lot of foreigners here!'

Celebration is the only word to describe
        the experience,
When L'Arche arrived the next day, we were
on hand to welcome them. Then together
we met the groups from La Merci and the
dancing began!

It was a meeting without barriers. We
had travelled to join the 12,000 persons
who came from 18 countries to share life.
Of the pilgrims, 4,000 were mentally retarded.

We prayed in the Basilica.
We danced in the square.
Those unable to walk were assisted by friends,
        brothers who had the strength.
We sang in the hotels, met in the pubs.
We performed at the fiesta in the rain that we
        scarcely noticed, so great was our joy.
We shared our sweaters,
        our raincoats,
        candy bars and cameras.
We shared this brief moment of our lives,
and we learned the meaning of Pilgrimage;
        the rich and the poor,
        travelling together,
        sharing hardships and joys,
        and learning prayer
        and brotherhood.

"I will never forget, for example,
the half hour spent with the
three pilgrims from Yugoslavia.
We had no common language, yet
what a marvellous meeting of hearts!
Brenda had to be fed from her mother's
hand, (no fork for fear of hurting
the badly deformed little body that
was never still), unable to speak,
and with hands totally paralysed,
she expressed her joy with a
fantastic smile and by clapping
her feet together.
She spoke,
with beautiful finesse,
the language of the heart.
This language, she taught to others.
But we, who have such a facile
use of words, can quickly forget.

With beautiful, confident freedom,
Harold went up to the pulpit at the
grotto,
took the microphone from the unsuspecting
priest, and announced to the thousands
assembled,

'There are three people here from
Cobourg, Canada; Jim and Mary Clarke
and me. Also, the whole gang from
Daybreak is here!'

It was only right that everyone should know.

So many thousands of suffering people,
        with crippled bodies,
        or crippled minds
        or crippled hearts.
Yet the whole experience was one of
        joyful celebration.
It was an overwhelming sign,
        a living proof,
that Jesus is risen."
        (Father Bill Clarke, Letters of L'Arche)

Pere Dominic

A picnic at Asha Niketan meant sending a postcard to
the monks to say we were coming for the day and
arriving for the picnic before the postcard!

The monks' surprise was obvious as we straggled to
their doorstep, but they recovered sufficiently to offer
us water and a shady spot to eat.

Then Père Dominic spotted us. Obviously happy at our
presence, he welcomed us with extraordinary warmth
and invited us into the monastery for more water
and fruit.

For siesta, we chose the front steps of the monastery.
The expressions of some of the monks as they came
out and almost tripped over the series of bodies
were beautiful!

Once refreshed, Father Dominic and some of the
brothers joined us for more sweets. Then we departed,
sad to leave the new friends we had made.

The boys, with their few words of English, told us —
'Fun' and 'Go back.'

The amazing thing was our deep identity with their
sentiments. For such a simple outing, we said to
        each other,
'Good time.'

A picnic at
Asha Niketan – Bangalore

"In India we have thousands of people
        who are hungry.
In one of our houses in Calcutta,
        our Sisters daily cook
        for four thousand people,
and the day we don't cook,
        they have nothing to eat.

During the trouble in India,
        when many of our brothers and sisters
        of the same father
        came to India from Pakistan,
these beautiful Indian friends told me,
        'Mother, don't cook for us today.
        Give our food to them.'
For them, it meant going without food
        that day."
                                (Mother Teresa)

In the streets of Bombay

Some children in England
    pay for the flour.
Some in Australia
    pay to transport it.
A Hindu baker in Calcutta
    bakes and delivers to the Sisters
    one thousand loaves of bread
    every day.
Children in Denmark
    provide money for milk.
Some in Germany
    supply the vitamins.

'Is not this the fast that I choose . . .
Is it not to share your bread with the
    hungry?'
                (Isaiah 58)

The loaves are taken from
    the large wooden tea crates,
packed into cloth bags and carried by the Sisters
    to their brothers.

Families, visited in the vast slum areas,
    receive bread.

Slum children, at school have bread
    at recess time.

The lepers, whose day it is for treatment
    receive clean bandages, vitamins,
    and bread for the day.

Those resting on the mats in the House of the Dying,
    receive bread.

Young girls, learning to sew or type or read,
    receive bread.

The handicapped and abandoned children
    receive bread.

Novices prepare the bread – Calcutta

"To feed the poor is not an answer to the problem.
We are here today,
     filling the gap.

Tomorrow, the needs arise again."
(Brother Andrew)

It is vain to try to fill the gap.
The needs
     will never be satisfied.

It is the age old problem.

The Missionaries know this,
     especially those
who have been working for
     twenty years or more.

They have dedicated their lives
     to something which,
humanly speaking,
     can never be done.

Waiting for school to begin

"I don't know the future
     but to me, today,
when a life comes into my hands,
all my love and my energy goes
     to support that life,
     to help that life to grow
     to its fullness,
because this person has been created
     in the image of God.

We have no right to destroy that life."
                              (Mother Teresa)

"A mentally retarded person
    can lead a deeply sensitive life,
a life of the heart,
    which tends to draw him
    into close relationships
    with other persons
and by which he can be protected,
    guided and encouraged
along the path of
    human and spiritual progress.

The mentally retarded person,
    much like the primitive man
is essentially a person
    of heart
    and of deep sensitivity."
                                    (Jean Vanier)

Pat and Francois at breakfast —
La Promesse, Pierrefonds

Soma Sundra unrolls the mats into a
large square on the porch in India.
Peggy sets the tables in the new house
at Daybreak in Canada.
Debby tries to find room for one more,
another visitor or friend at L'Arche.
We move in on the bench at Katimavik
in Cognac.

Unquestionable, meals are the moment
when one experiences the unique unity
in each foyer. One who is merely
looking, might miss the point. But
for anyone who has worked with, or
walked with or prayed with the men
and women around the table,
there is a deeper meaning.

*Dinner at
Asha Niketan –
Bangalore*

*Coffee Break
at La Promesse*

Daybreak has welcomed me many times. What
is touching to observe is the growing
capacity of the men and women to express
themselves. In the past, so silent and
tense, John is now trying to make conversation. Frank makes a five-minute speech
after his birthday supper and though we don't
always get the words, we listen to his word
of appreciation.

There is something profound in being simple
enough and having time enough to share
joyfully the events of the day in conversation.
It produces a security and a feeling of
belonging.

Relaxed, accepted, even the visitor is free
to observe how readily the men in India
share an orange for dessert, or how Annie
at Daybreak, will pass George's plate before
her own. Pierrot, in Trosly automatically
cuts Maxim's meat because he can't do it himself. And Patrick at Cognac responds to Jacqueline's
compliment on the good lunch he helped to
prepare. Also one observes Raphael's look
of tenderness across the table for one who
is temporarily distressed.

It's hard to describe but this experience of sharing
        our very food and ourselves,
is somehow linked mysteriously to another Supper,
        long ago.

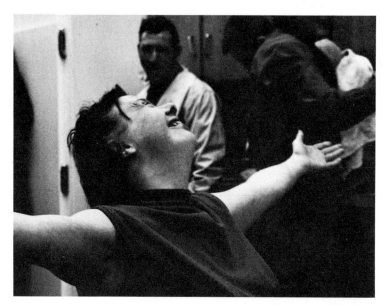

Helen at Daybreak –
Richmond Hill,
Ontario, Canada

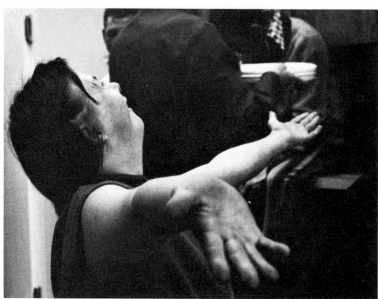

Holidays for Daybreak last year
    meant camping in Algonquin Park.
A daily routine,
    cleaning the campsite,
    washing in the lake,
    swimming or relaxing in the sun
was interrupted only by the arrival of friends
    who knew we were there and dropped by to
    see how we were surviving.

For the most part, we were good campers
although it wasn't to be everyone's
    cup of tea.

Helen feared so much walking from the
    immediate campsite,
because she had encountered a mouse on her
first day at camp. But certain facilities
necessitated the 'journey through the grass.'

For the most part of each day,
    she had only one thing on her mind,
and when it became necessary to take that walk,
    she would look frantically for me,
    explaining each time,
'You know Sue, I'm afraid of that mouse!'

One evening at supper, Steve and Anne saw
a large bear, wandering on the edge of the woods.
Steve quietly announced that if we were quiet and
looked, we would see a bear, at which point chaos
happened in the form of yells and screams of delight
and fear. The bear quickly disappeared.

I turned to Helen. 'Did you see him?', I asked.
'Yes,' she answered, and went on without stopping,
'but you'll come with me tonight, won't you, Sue.
You know, I'm afraid of that mouse!'

Malcolm Muggeridge, author of
Something Beautiful for God,
a book about Mother Teresa,
remarked to me,
'The incredible thing is, that Mother
Teresa has no time to read the news or
watch TV, yet she can sense the trouble
spots in the world and see the nature
of the healings necessary.'

Late last year, Mother Teresa conceived the idea
        of a community in Belfast.
She contacted some Anglican Sisters,
        a Presbyterian lady,
        and some Baptist Mission Sisters
who agreed to share a house with the missionaries
        and pray together,
        live together,
        and work for unity in Belfast.

Some missionaries went to make beginnings
        and difficulties arose.
Efforts to begin together met staunch opposition
        from Catholic and Protestant sectors.
Misunderstandings became a source of suffering,
        and the community, as invisioned
        never became a reality.
Mother Teresa commented to me about this endeavour:
'The Belfast Community will be good.
There has been so much suffering and failure.
It is like the life of Jesus.
The efforts of so many people will bear much fruit
        for unity.'

Since that time, there has been a small breakthrough.
        The missionaries, in the Catholic sector,
        and the Anglican Sisters in the Protestant sector
        have begun to share their work.
Conscious of the division, because they live apart,
        but coming together for work,
        they signify hope.

Mother Teresa – Dum Dum

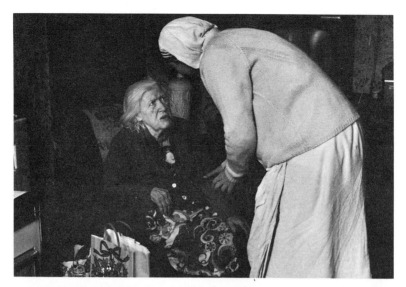

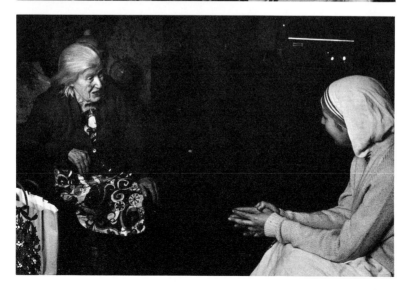

In London, England the Sisters, some co-workers
and friends operate a house for destitute women.
Sister Frederick summarized it.

> 'There isn't very much we can do.
> The girls have suffered a great deal.
> We could never understand the depths
> of their sufferings. Our house
> is only a temporary shelter until
> they can get on their feet, maybe
> get work, and find a place to stay.
> We simply try to welcome them
> and to make this house,
> a house of love.
>
> The women themselves help us to
> operate the house. Each gives in
> time and talent according to her
> ability and the state of her health.
> So many broken lives!
>
> Somehow they hear about us. Some
> ring the doorbell or some are
> brought by police or friends. Some-
> one who has been here may bring
> another who is without a place.'

'Would you not rather be with the very poor in
Calcutta?' I asked Sister. 'Isn't that why
you became a Missionary?'

'There is a deeper poverty here,' she answered.
'This loneliness, this anguish of despair!'
Then with such beautiful simplicity, she added,
> 'This is my India.'

The House for the Destitute – London, England.

In the slums of Rome, Italy

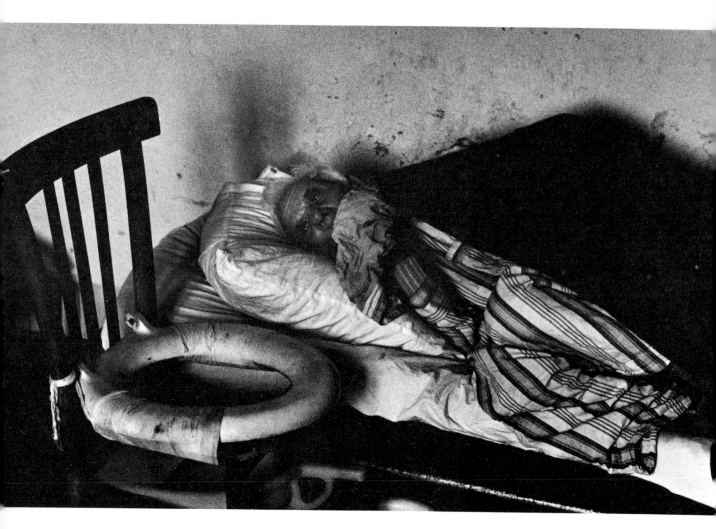

"In Australia with the Aborigines the Sisters
visit the people
I entered a terrible small place
with an old man,
sitting in this very dirty place.
And I told him,
    'allow me to clean your place?'
he kept on saying,
    'I'm all right, I'm all right.'
And I said to him,
    'but you will be more all right if you let me
    clean your place.'
Then at the end, he allowed me.
There I found a lamp,
    covered with dirt
and he told me,
    'a long time I have not lighted that lamp.'
I asked him,
    'why did you not light your lamp?'
and he said,
    'for whom?
    nobody wants me
    I have no one to visit me.
    I have no one to light the lamp for . . .'
and I asked him one more question,
    'will you light the lamp every evening
    if the Sisters come?'
and he answered, 'yes.'
From that day he has kept his word.
    He lights the lamp,
    and when the Sisters don't come,
    he imagines they have come,
    so he continues to light his lamp.

The other day the Sisters sent me word,
    your friend sends greetings and says that
    there is a new light in his life,
    beginning the day he lighted his lamp
    after so many years . . .''
                           (Mother Teresa)

The Missionaries of Charity work in Italy,
      in England and Jordan,
      in Australia and Ireland,
      in United States, South America,
      and Bangladesh,
      in Africa and Ceylon,
giving whole-hearted, free service
      to the poorest of the poor.

Soon to be opened in each country is
      a house of prayer.
Sisters unable to serve with washing and
      feeding,
      will serve in another way.

School for poor children – Rome

Debby and Raphael –
L'Arche, Trosly Breuil

"Could it happen that the assistant
        to the retarded man, discovers
that he, too, is handicapped?
That he, too, needs someone,
        some mysterious power of love
to break the chains of egoism
        which have amputated his powers
        to love,
        share,
        listen,
        receive?

Each of the communities of L'Arche is essentially
        one community,
        where assistants and assisted
        mingle together
        calling forth each other;
each with his qualities,
each with his limits,
        accepting each other,
        growing together.

And thus, bonds deepen and community rises."
                                    (Jean Vanier)

Huffy helps Christian

The core of L'Arche,
        without any doubt,
revolves around the Beatitudes.

Living with the retarded, who are endowed richly
        in the area of the affections,
there is an awakening of the deeper meaning
in the words,

        Blessed are the poor.

Pam, an assistant, had this to say:

'When I first came to Trosly,
    I was going to do so much.
I wanted to work hard, and help, and show
    what I could do.
Gradually I discovered that there was really
    little I could do.
I couldn't use all my knowledge.
The boys didn't even notice how smart I was.

It was hard until the day I realized
    that they were glad I was here,
    just so we could be together.
It wasn't what I could do.
They liked me,
    just me.'

In the chapel – Trosly

Isabelle, Jean Pierre,
Maurice – Pierrefonds

Agnes was encouraged by a sense of solidarity
with all the others, when she returned last March
from the first meeting of L'Arche International.

With Adrianno, her husband, she has undergone a
period of staunch opposition by her parents, who
would like the couple to settle down to a 'normal'
life.

Instead, they've 'settled' on a large farm in
southwest France. They initially opened a work
centre for thirty day workers from the surrounding
villages, but now they have welcomed permanent
brothers from homes and hospitals nearby to live
in the two foyers which have been fixed over.

'It's the boys and the girls who create the atmosphere
of life and hope here,' she says. 'Also I know, now
that we are not alone. In some mysterious way, the
discovery that we are linked to Steve and Ann in
Canada, to Therese, Geoff and Anne in England,
to Gabrielle, Ron and Judy in India, and to all our
brothers and sisters in Trosly, this is a big source of
strength for me.'

The kitchen at La Promesse

'Maurice and I want to share our love.
It's wonderful to be part of the gradual
improvement of these men because when
they smile, you feel they have been
reborn. When things get hard, we try
to help each other. Each night before
retiring we renew together our marriage
vows and we pray together.'

Although Mary, a nurse, had been to L'Arche
earlier, she returned to North America
to rediscover, in the light of her experience,
the values of the society in which
she was raised. She married Maurice, an M.A.
in special education for the deaf and
lived a year in the States before returning
to France to open a foyer for the more
deeply handicapped men. Next year they
plan to go to Ottawa to take responsibility
for a community there.

I asked Maurice, 'What makes people stay
when things are hard? If they are free,
why don't they go?'

'Some do go,' he answered. 'But this is
a call for persons thirsting for community
and a simple way of life. There comes
a point when one accepts to go on because
the call of love is so strong.'

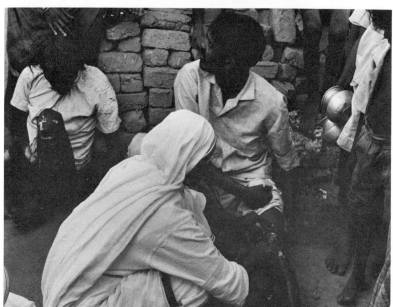

*The lepers
in Bangalore,
India*

"There are 47,000 lepers in India and elsewhere
        that the Sisters touch in love
        and serve.
These are the people
        who are not wanted.

Leprosy is a terrible disease;
it disfigures people.
It makes them look so terrible.
Yet,
they are very lovable people.

We have mobile clinics
        and we go to them.
We do not ask them to come to us,
        they are scorned and rejected,
        sometimes they are unable to walk.

When they see the young Sisters
        coming with a smile,
        taking care of them,
        singing for them,
they feel there is someone
        in all this world
        who cares.
We cannot heal their disease,
        but we can make them feel
        that they are wanted."
                                (Mother Teresa)

The lepers coming for treatment

The first sight of the leper
        in his crowded slum
        could be
I say, could be,
        a devastating experience.

But Sister Clare hastens
        to meet her friends
and the outsider with her
        is drawn into a circle
        of welcome
        of friends.

The disease is unpleasant; the odour, the heat, the flies
but the lepers
        are incredible people.
Their faces are sad,
their eyes sad,
        yet peaceful,
        deeply accepting,
        yet continually made aware of
        death.

They hasten to find chairs
        in an area where there are no chairs
        only shacks,
        some few pots and pans,
        rags.
        And they invite the outsiders to sit down,
        because in the course of the afternoon,
        many hundreds of friends will line up
to receive clean dressings on their sores,
pills, and encouragement.

The Sisters smile
and listen
and are deeply present
        for those few brief moments
showing no sign of the revulsion
which they must experience.

The lepers are patient
        waiting
        anticipating the meeting
sometimes it is in conversation
sometimes in silence
mostly in an extraordinary peace.

"One week we had no money to buy bandages,
so we didn't go to the lepers.
The next week, when we went, they said to us:
    'why didn't you come to us?'
We told them that we had no bandages.
    'we don't care if you haven't any bandages,'
    they told us,
    'we missed you.
Will you promise to come,
even if you have no bandages'."
(Sister Clare)

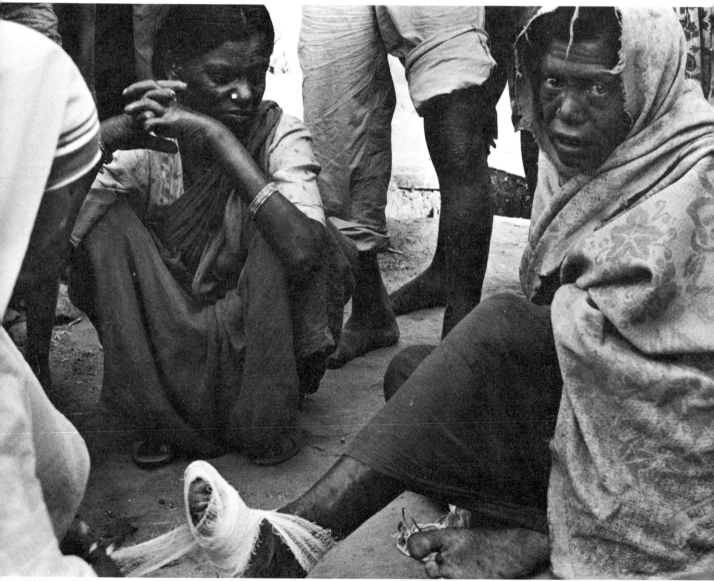

Sister Francesca and her team in Calcutta
 have medical charts for 15,000 lepers.
They try to see each one, once a month.
Sister has worked with the lepers for 22 years.
She speaks of them as her friends, with compassion.

"One day the landowner, came and burnt their houses
down. I hurried out to the site and I invited them
 to come to the compound where the Sisters live,
 to stay with us until we could find another place.
Although they had so little to lose in that fire
 they were very sad,
so I promised them although I was very young
 and had no grounds for doing so,
I promised them, on the spot
 that I would find them a place
 that would be their own.
The landowner would never burn them out again.

The next day, I knew I must set out to look,
 but I didn't know where,
so one of my friends came with me and
 we set out down the road.
Soon a car stopped and a gentleman asked us,
 'where are you going?'
When I told him we were looking for land for the lepers,
he asked:
 'how much do you need?'
I didn't know why he was asking,
 nor did I know how much land would be needed,
so I said:
 'how much can you give?'
He took us and showed us a property,
 asked if it was suitable,
 and gave it to us.
By lunch time that day, I had 35 acres for my people.

Now, there is a hospital on the site
 and about 5,000 lepers live there."
       (Sister Francesca)

A Sister ministers to the lepers

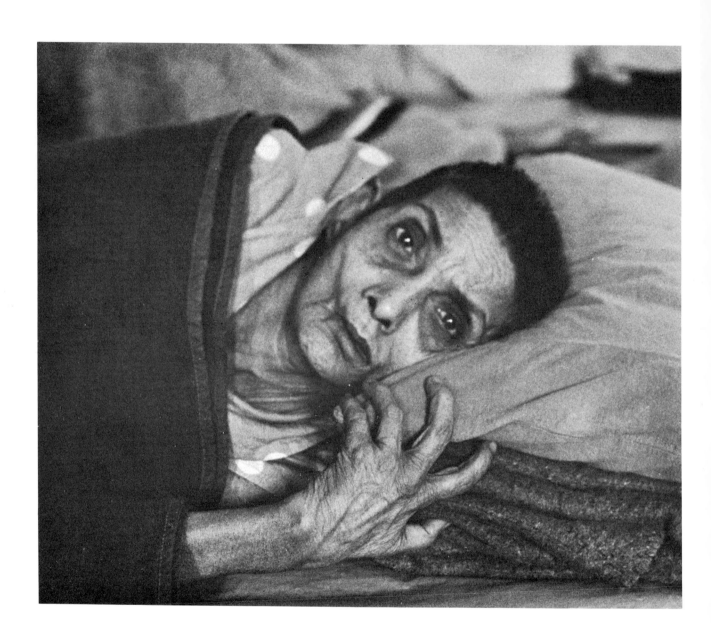

'The interesting thing is that
        the leper has called forth Mother Teresa.
When the rich man closes himself off,
        because of the fight in his human heart between
        possessions and love,
and when he enters into the world of egoism,
one sees
        in spite of all the economic stability,
death in his face.'

'Are you saying that we should always have
        the miserable ones with us
so they can call forth Mother Teresa?'

'I will die some day, and so will you.
On my deathbed,
        I will be miserable.
I will need . . .
I will need Mother Teresa.''
                (Jean Vanier, CBC show Man Alive,
                'Love has no Doubts',
                  to Patrick Watson)

The House of the Dying – Madras

*The Community of L'Arche
at prayer — Trosly — Ange, Debby, Jean and Jean*

Michel, from Le Val, suffers
        a mental deficiency,
but even more, he suffers the wound
        of physical disfigurement.
He is a man who knows
        and has lived,
        rejection.

He and Père Thomas are fast friends.
The Père has done much to help Michel
to integrate his handicaps.

One Sunday, not long ago,
        at the Community prayer meeting,
Michel's prayer haltingly broke the silence.
'Lord, help me to accept myself the way I am.'

The Community of Asha Niketan
at prayer – Bangalore

"Community can only be created
and nurtured and strengthened
by the deep, transforming power
        of the Holy Spirit . . .
Humanly speaking, this is not possible."
                        (Jean Vanier)

Before lunch at Cognac,
After supper in the foyer in Trosly,
Before supper at the main house
        in Canada.
Early morning and early evening
        in the prayer room in India,
The communities of L'Arche gather
        to pray.

There may be a reading or a song.
Generally there is spontaneous prayer
        or traditional prayer
        or silence.
There is no formula.

Not everyone comes.
There is the freedom of the
        sons and daughters of God.
But it is so beautiful!

Christians of different denominations.
        In India,
Christians and non-Christians
        praying together.

My Brother   My Sister

Just as you and I are unique
    human beings,
So too, are Jean Vanier and Mother Teresa.

Just as there is within us,
    the ability to share,
So there is in
    Jean, our brother
    and
    Mother, our sister.

If we put them in a 'special' category,
    push them up and out of reach,
we have failed to grasp the essential mystery.

'God chose what is foolish in the world
    to shame the wise,
God chose what is weak in the world
    to confound the strong.'
(Corinthians, 1:27)

Our Brother